Cocooning Lifestyle:

Enjoying Happy and Safe Times at Home

By Tess Jansen

About this book:

What does Cocooning mean? Who invented Cocooning? What are the benefits and pleasures of a Cocooning lifestyle for me?

Discover answers to these questions and many more from another book by Tess Jansen who already wrote about Niksen - The Power of Doing Nothing.

A Cocooning lifestyle is a great help in times when you want to stay safely and happily at home. This book will show you the benefits and give you ideas on how to spend a great time at home, enjoy the benefits of de-stressing, and also of using gained additional time and freedom. Cocooning does not mean to be alone or even lonely! Even though this can be part of it, there are many ways to connect to other people.

Cocooning Lifestyle: Enjoying Happy and Safe Times at Home

By Tess Jansen

"A person who has not left home for a long time may know a lot more about the outside world as compared to a person who commutes to work daily."

Cocooning Lifestyle:

Enjoying Happy and Safe Times at Home

BN Publishing

© 2020 by Tess Jansen, Zürich

ISBN: 978- 5454036898

TABLE OF CONTENTS

- INTRODUCTION 7
- WHAT IS COCOONING LIFESTYLE? 10
  - Cocooning lifestyle 13
  - The background and history of cocooning 16
  - The seasonal effect 20
- DIFFERENT TYPES OF COCOONING 23
  - Different types of cocooning 25
  - Different lifestyles that suit cocooning 30
    - Hygge 30
    - Lagom 34
    - Niksen 37
    - Coorie 40
- ACTIVITIES TO TRY AT HOME 43
  - Productivity 45
  - Entertainment 47
  - Hobbies 49
  - Social life 52
  - Cocooning lifestyle: a summary 55
- CONCLUSION 59
- More Books by Tess Jansen 62

INTRODUCTION

When you wrap newborn babies in a sheet, they sleep a lot more peacefully. It makes them feel like they're being held lovingly. This feeling comes from having a protective cover around themselves.

Creating a layer of comfort and safety around yourself can do wonders for your mental wellbeing. Whether we're talking about filtering out negative thoughts and ideas or building boundaries to protect yourself, self-protection can transform your personality. It is quite reassuring to know that you're in a safe zone.

The concept of cocooning does not only require you to protect yourself from physical harm. It calls for a complete abandonment of activities that are harmful to your mental peace. Most of us would agree that this is best done by staying at home and avoiding to meet too many people.

When you say it so bluntly, the idea may appear somewhat unpleasant. It makes you feel like you're being too rebellious or unreasonable. But the fact is, we're all practicing cocooning in one way or the other without realizing it.

However, we're unable to avail the complete benefits because we're not totally familiar with the concept. Call it a lack of awareness or a reluctance to admit the reality, we're not completely honest about our lifestyle choices. We tend to make excuses instead of making it known to people that we prefer to stay indoors.

Cocooning can be turned into a beautiful life experience that nourishes the mind and soul. There are no hard and fast rules and you can design a routine that suits you best. You may even suggest cocooning to somebody who is in dire need of stress relief.

As long as the ultimate purpose is achieved, i.e. you work on your happiness and contentment, it doesn't matter what activities you choose for your indoor lifestyle. But it would be nice to have some guidance when you're getting started. Hence, in the following text, we aim to provide all the necessary information that you may need to make your cocooning lifestyle more effective.

You may be aware that some animals hibernate during the winters. When the environment doesn't suit them and they need to preserve their energy, they don't leave their homes for the entire season. As human beings, we can definitely take a leaf out of their book.

Our reasons to seek isolation may be a little more complex, but we need to reassure ourselves that it is completely okay to feel this way. You are the best judge of what your mind and body need. If it tells you to take a step back from the current routine, you must obey.

And cocooning isn't even as dramatic as it may seem in the beginning. However, the positive effects sure are quite extraordinary. There is an immense amount of self-discovery and character enhancement that takes place while cocooning.

───────────────

WHAT IS COCOONING LIFESTYLE?

The outside world is buzzing with hustle and bustle. Everyone is rushing to reach their destination with little time to stop and catch a breath. Even 'relaxation' has taken a different meaning in recent times.

In most cases, you're expected to reach a place at a set time, chit chat for a bit, and then get back to business. If you sit and think about it, the idea doesn't seem too refreshing. In fact, it seems far from it.

Any activity that is meant for relaxation should be free of rules imposed by others. Whether it is a movie outing with friends or dining out with your colleagues, you're expected to adhere to certain protocols. These gatherings mostly leave you drained instead of providing relaxation.

Whenever you want to unwind, your first thought should be to go home. The place where you reside should be your biggest source of comfort. On the contrary, people seek an escape from home whenever they wish to lighten up.

Mental peace eludes those who seek it in the external world. To find distractions is futile because whenever you run out of new outdoor activities to try, you will fall back into despair. Until and unless you become comfortable with solitude and your permanent abode, you will keep running around in circles to find happiness.

The most profound form of joy and happiness comes from being self-sufficient. Depending on others for your own mental wellbeing is a dangerous trait. If your friends bail out on a plan, it should never make you feel miserable.

Of course, it is much easier to say this as compared to actually doing it. But changing your lifestyle gradually can enable you to be solely responsible for your own happiness. One of the most relevant lifestyles in this regard is cocooning.

When somebody spends too much time at home, we say that he/she stays holed up in a cocoon. In retrospect, we all secretly wish to have a lifestyle that allows us to just be ourselves, without caring about other peoples' validation. A lifestyle that is free of artificial meetups, just to appease our peers.

It wouldn't be wrong to say that a large section of the world has gone from mocking the preference to stay at home to desiring such a lifestyle for itself. As you grow older, you realize the importance of preserving your mental peace no matter what it requires. And what better way to do that than making your home so comfortable that you never need to go out in order to replenish your energies.

───────────────

Cocooning lifestyle

The literal meaning of cocoon is a protective covering. The most broadly known definition is a silky case that is spun by the larvae of various insects for protection during the time as pupae. A cocooning lifestyle is no different.

It involves staying sheltered in one's home, protected from all kinds of potential dangers and negativity. People who are cocooning seldom leave home and adjust their lifestyle in a way that requires minimum outside trips. It takes some effort to make this possible but once you're able to manage all the facilities, it is definitely worth it.

There is always some part of the house that makes you feel safer and more comfortable than the rest of the areas. It could be your room, the attic, the roof, or any place where you can just breathe freely and completely be yourself. Whenever you want to find some peace, you head to this particular area.

The idea of cocooning is to extend this feeling of comfort to the entire house. Home should feel like a safe haven. When you're inside, you should find comfort in the knowledge that whatever is happening outside cannot tamper with your peace. Let's try another example. Sometimes, you plug in your earphones and increase the volume to drown out the noise of the surroundings. You listen to your favorite music or anything that is soothing to feel calmer.

When you do this, you're creating a cocoon for yourself mentally. You enter a zone where nothing and nobody can disturb your peace. That is what a cocooning lifestyle requires you to do.

Being able to stay inside the comfort of your home, in your own bubble of happiness is nothing short of a luxury. Some definitions called this practice spending 'leisure' time at home and we couldn't agree more. Cocooning is not about locking yourself in an enclosed space like it is some kind of punishment.

Preferring online shopping over market trips, ordering in instead of dining out, inviting close friends at home rather than hanging out at a club are all examples of a cocooning lifestyle. Basically, anything that enables you to minimize one on one interaction (with strangers in particular) can be considered a part of this concept. It is all about spending valuable time at home and avoid stressful obligations.

Luckily, this has been made very convenient by technology. You can manage practically everything from home without much trouble. The e-commerce sector is thriving and for most products and services, you just have to pick up the phone and order.

———————————

The background and history of cocooning

You may have noticed that most geniuses in history were not very social people. This is because (according to research) people who are more intelligent do not like to socialize much. Be it Einstein or Newton, many iconic historic figures were known to be introverts.

But every interaction that someone had with them left that person mesmerized by their thoughtful insights. It seems like limited interaction improved the quality of their exchanges. Maybe this was due to all the time they spent alone, just contemplating about various subjects.

This is not to say that extroverts may be less intelligent or that cocooning is not meant for them. You can be an extrovert and still dislike interactions that serve no purpose. It is just about preferring a relaxed, wholesome lifestyle over a rushed, chaotic one.

Forced conversations have made us much less insightful. From day to day interactions with work colleagues to attending a party with some old friends, we're just concerned with exchanging pleasantries and carrying out small talk. This is due to various reasons.

Firstly, life has become extremely busy and robotic. People have little time to introspect and this reflects in their social demeanor. Taunts, sarcasm, and negative comments have increased because everyone is increasingly displeased with life in general.

This is probably the biggest reason that has made the idea of meeting people seem so exhausting. You dread any impending social event because you already know what kind of conversations you'll get to hear. It bothers you even more if you're not a confrontational person.

The second reason is the increased amount of stress which has had a negative impact on our overall mental health. We're no longer interested in investing time and energy in expanding our social circle. We're more content with connections that require minimal effort.

In the past few decades, there was an excess of social activity. As the world shrunk into a global village and the communication systems became more convenient, the list of acquaintances grew immensely. There were more social events, attended by a larger number of people.

While this was great for everyone's personal and professional prospects, it also exhausted the emotional health gradually. When you get to know a wider variety of people, you have all kinds of different experiences. Some are pleasantly surprising while others turn out to be quite a disappointment.

The urge to cocoon could be considered a way to detox after tolerating a lot of toxic trends. This is similar to when the overuse of social media makes you wish for some quiet time on your own. The human mind and body are designed to naturally balance excessive activity with adequate rest.

But we often deny this urge for various reasons. For example, we're okay with compromising our health in order to excel at work. We do not want to miss social obligations due to the fear of missing out or being left behind.

Moreover, there is this myth that cocooning is for people who have some serious trouble leaving home. This would include those who are chronically ill as well as the elderly. Although cocooning definitely suits the vulnerable section of the society more, it is kind of tailor-made for the younger generation as well.

For as long as we remember, we've lived in urban settlements. We're not inclined to fetch water from the well or have a stroll in the forest. We just want a house (with all the necessary facilities) that requires the least amount of effort from our side. Now, we're not equating the modern era day to day chores to the laborious tasks of the ancient times. We're just pointing out that ours is a spoilt generation. So we need a lifestyle that matches the laid back approach we have in life.

Cocooning is a term introduced by Faith Popcorn back in 1981. She is an author, futurist, and the founder (as well as CEO) of a marketing consultancy firm called BrainReserve. Popcorn is especially known for her brilliance in predicting future trends. She also wrote about different forms of cocooning, which we will discuss in a later section of the text. Cocooning gained momentum in the latter half of the 20th century and has been a popular idea ever since. As more people get familiarized with the idea, modifications and variations also increase.

The seasonal effect

If the idea of cocooning all through the year seems too extreme, you may choose to do it seasonally. The choice of the season you wish to spend indoors may depend on the harshness of weather during that time in your area. For example, if your area gets a lot of snowfall and winters are particularly hard, you may choose to spend that time indoors. If you think about cocooning in winters, your idea would be to have a warm, cozy, and comfortable place to live in. It could be freezing cold outside and the thought of being wrapped in a blanket, maybe enjoying a hot beverage would seem extremely tempting to anybody. The snowfall may be a very pleasing sight but it would be even better if you can get to enjoy it from inside the window.

Winters are generally known to make people lazy. The level of physical activity declines in cold weather, probably because of less blood circulation. One feels inclined to stay in bed or relax on the couch instead of going out.

You could sit near the fireplace and read a book, watch something relaxing on television, or simply treat yourself to a delicious meal. Doing something for your happiness while cocooning is relatively easier. Besides, the holiday season also coincides with the winter season in many parts of the world.

On the other hand, cocooning in summers would be a completely different experience altogether. You would want to save yourself from the scorching heat by staying indoors, preferably in a pleasant, air-conditioned room. Your preference might change with the season but the desire to stay comfortably indoors always remains.

In summers, you would think about keeping yourself well-hydrated and fresh. Going outside in hot weather can be pretty exhausting. Your skin also faces the effects of the heat.

Talking about the skin, you might have felt that when you rejoin school or work after a few holidays, you tend to look a lot fresher. The wind in winters makes your skin dry while in summers, it starts looking a bit oily. Of course, this varies according to the skin type too but with cocooning, you can at least prevent weather-related skin issues.

The lifestyle can be molded according to the season. In fact, that is what we do whether we're cocooning or not. We bring out the warm clothes in winters and quickly get the summer bods ready as soon as the weather changes.

The difference with cocooning is that everything would be done without leaving home. You can order products and services online and stock up for the entire season. Once you become used to it, the lifestyle starts to seem like a natural choice.

It is just like drawing the curtains when you need to get some sun and replace them when you don't. You only need minor, one-off adjustments when a season begins. Otherwise, most of our homes are already designed to have full functionality regardless of the weather.

DIFFERENT TYPES OF COCOONING

Mental health has never been as fragile as it is in recent times. An increasing number of people are suffering from chronic anxiety and depression. Due to this, the general level of physical health is also declining.

There are various therapies and medications that are being tried out to counter this rising menace. But these are more like short-term measures that provide temporary relief. In order to recover from the aforementioned mental health issues completely, we need to eliminate their root causes.

Stress can be caused by multiple reasons for different people. Some are worried about work or finances while others are going through a rough patch in their personal relationships. Whatever the reason for people's anxiety may be, there's always one common denominator: the fear of uncertainty.

Uncertainty is increased due to the matters that are beyond our control. We can control our own actions but we can't accurately predict others' reactions towards the same. No amount of cautiousness will make us determine future outcomes beforehand.

The everyday routine involves various factors that add to the feeling of anxiety. Social behaviors, the traffic on the roads, work issues, almost everything that we're supposed to deal with is inherently unpredictable by nature. So, one can't help but feel absolutely drained by the end of the day.

We can decrease stress in our lives greatly if we create a routine that relies very little on other people. You won't have to deal with reaching your workplace late because someone else's car broke down in the middle of the road. You won't spend the entire day feeling bad about an unpleasant situation you witnessed at work.

When you're cocooning, you have to deal with fewer people, be part of stressful situations less often, and can ensure minimizing the overall level of uncertainty in your life. In short, the lifestyle can potentially be the solution to most of your mental health issues. This is why cocooning is not just a luxurious choice but the need of the hour as well.

Different types of cocooning

As mentioned in the previous chapter, Faith Popcorn wrote about different forms of cocooning. She did not only familiarize the world with the upcoming trend many years ago but also had a close idea of the ways this concept may take shape. Popcorn has written extensively about such topics. She also introduced three subcategories of cocooning i.e armored cocoon, wandering cocoon, and socialized cocoon.

Armored cocoon

Armored cocoon refers to a lifestyle in which people create and an extra layer of security around themselves. In this form of cocooning, there are additional measures like high-tech security gates, alarm systems, weapons for protection, etc. So we're not just talking about staying comfortable, but we're also practically ensuring a foolproof security system.

This sounds more suitable for areas with a volatile security situation. If the law and order conditions are too worrisome or there are threats like a military attack or terrorism, you would definitely want to upgrade your security system. Staying home is just one aspect of staying safe in such circumstances.

Nowadays there are gated communities that provide extra security to the residents. There are even rules and regulations to enter and exit the place. Identity checks are performed at the entry points which reduces the chances of any unauthorized (or fishy) person getting in.

We've often seen in movies or tv shows that when a scientist is working on something secretive he/she chooses a secluded part of the house/lab. There are layers and layers of security. They have alarm systems that go off if someone tries to breach the security.

These scenes from thrillers are one thing, we've even seen how Dexter from Dexter's Laboratory kept his lab confidential. It was a well-hidden secret from the rest of the world (except his annoying sister). The young boy was portrayed as somebody who isn't too fond of having too many visitors.

While generally people cocooning do not have such a dramatic secret to keep, they can still identify with some of the ideas. The only thing they're trying to protect is their mental peace and happiness. A well-guarded, secretive lifestyle may make people feel more secure and hence help in achieving this goal.

<u>Wandering cocoon</u>

Solo drives can be a very liberating experience. Going on a long drive is often a good way of relieving all day's stress and exhaustion. When worries consume you and the routine life seems too overwhelming, you just feel like hitting the road with no particular destination in mind.

To spend most of your time traveling with little or no company is an example of a wandering cocoon. You may attend most matters by phone, eat while on the go, and basically have your life revolve around your travels. The facilities that automobile companies are providing lately also signal towards this trend. But this may not sound too practical for many people. A more easily conceivable idea would be something like container homes, which have become quite a trend lately. This too is a form of the wandering cocoon lifestyle.

The term wandering cocoon gives you a lot of nomadic vibes. To be on the road with all the essentials and settle wherever you feel like was something exclusive to the nomads. Now it is being practiced by the most technologically advanced sections of society as well.

A wanderer does not need much to survive. He/she can eat from any place on the roadside, can sleep in the car, and manage work and personal affairs by phone. The constant change of environment is refreshing and the reluctance to deal with acquaintance also doesn't remain an issue anymore. Of course, there are some prerequisites for this lifestyle. For example, whether you have enough finances to afford such living, is your health stable enough, is it possible for you to ensure the smooth operation of work, etc. But if the answers to most of such questions are positive, there is nothing better than this luxury.

<u>Socialized cocoon</u>

This form of cocooning is the most practical and the most relevant one in recent times. It's just about staying private and what the current generation calls 'low-key'. You just simply stay at home most of the time and to avoid complete social isolation, invite friends over occasionally.

If you are living alone, then you already enjoy a significant amount of privacy. The feeling of having a comfortable and secure den already exists. All you need to do is figure out a way to leave home less often and avoid unnecessary visitors. However, if you share the residence with friends or family, you'll have to be more creative with cocooning. You may insulate the room or divide the place to have some private area. Alternatively, if you're comfortable enough, you may perceive the whole apartment/house and the people you live with a part of your social cocoon.

Earlier in the text, we mentioned that introverts may prefer cocooning more than extroverts. This may be even truer for socialized cocooning. It involves just staying indoors and not dealing with other people whatsoever.

Another aspect that we must mention here is the increasing levels of social anxiety. This is a serious problem and the patients experience symptoms like increased heart rate, shortness of breath, sweating, etc when they're around other people. Social cocooning may also be used to alleviate these symptoms until the problem is resolved completely.

Overall, this third type of cocooning is the most commonly practiced by people. While the other two require some significant arrangements to be made beforehand, this can be applied almost immediately without much effort. The positive effects also start showing very soon.

Different lifestyles that suit cocooning

There are some preexisting trends that can enhance the quality of your time spent indoors. Different countries have introduced lifestyle changes to deal with the increasing level of stress in our lives. We've picked some that are relevant to cocooning in the text below.

Hygge

Hygge is a Danish word that does not have a precise English variant. But it is generally defined as the feeling of comfort and coziness. The focus word here is 'feeling' and not the satisfaction we derive from something tangible.

The word finds its origin in the Norwegian language, meaning 'wellbeing'. Today it is a well-known Danish lifestyle intended to protect the same, i.e wellbeing. It is based on the idea of being present in a moment and enjoying it wholeheartedly.

If we're completely honest, this sounds rather vague and ordinary. But this is exactly what makes hygge a flexible way of happiness rather than something tiresome or time-consuming. It isn't about doing something extraordinary but learning to find contentment in ordinary actions.

Being unfamiliar with the language may make it a little tricky to understand the concept. For starters let's get on thing clear. Any product, service, or architecture promoted as being 'hygge' is nothing but a marketing gimmick.

Hygge is an intangible feeling which is hard to put into words, let alone translate into product and services. It has a deeper meaning which can only be felt and not learned. It requires moments of complete presence and not extensive efforts to find happiness.

For example, revisit the feeling of sitting by the window and enjoying the sound of rain. The moment when you light up a scented candle and just breathe in the aroma. Now tell us if you can precisely describe the feeling of such moments?

There is no defined list of such things. Experiencing the exact moment when a flower blooms, seeing a shooting star, listening to a baby's giggle are moments that make you feel more alive. They bring your attention back to the present moment.

Now refer to the description for hygge that we provided earlier. Being fully present in a moment makes it a lot more pleasant and memorable. Something so simple to do yet forgotten by the present generation.

Being more mindful of your own behavior would make you realize you're seldom completely there in the present moment. You're either worried about a future event or regretting something that happened in the past. Both serve little purpose in making the present feel better.

Let's learn a little more about the background of the hygge lifestyle. For those who don't know much about the country, Denmark receives very little sunlight (6 to 7 hours) in winters. So the evenings and nights constitute a major portion of the day.

Winters are generally associated with gloominess. The streets are quieter and the 'nightlife' isn't as happening as it is in summers. People prefer staying warm and cozy inside their homes.

So understandably, the people of Denmark had to do something to make their winters more cheerful. The tradition began with gathering around with your loved ones and enjoying a meal. Now hygge has a much broader meaning.

Since we're talking about hygge in the context of cocooning, we're more interested in the indoor activities. However, more than any practical step, hygge is about changing your perception of happiness. You can just sit down to read a book and consider it a part of the hygge lifestyle.

The moment you start associating positive feelings with ordinary, day to day actions, you begin living the hygge way. There could be plenty of flowers in your garden but you may not stop and admire their beauty too often. Doing such small, feel-good things habitually is what the Danish lifestyle entails.

Consider the example of a person who wakes up each morning and immediately looks for the phone to check the news or social media. He/she would probably end up in a bad mood due to all that is happening in the world these days. Thereon, it would be difficult to uplift the spirits and have a fulfilling day.

At first, this person would reluctantly drag him/herself out of bed and feel burdened by the entire routine ahead. The chores would seem too boring and tiresome and the spare time would be devoid of relaxation. In short, the whole day would be ruined.

On the other hand, let's consider someone with a completely different approach to starting a day. This person sets an alarm to witness the sunrise as soon as he/she wakes up. This is followed by a hot cup of coffee to enliven all the senses.

Now decide for yourself which of these two examples seems closer to the hygge lifestyles? So it isn't about taking drastic steps to feel happy. You just need to design your routine with a positive mindset.

To summarize it all, create an ambiance that makes you happy. Include simple, soulful activities in your routine. Enjoy the present moment instead of worrying about the past or future. Doing all this would automatically count as the hygge lifestyle.

Lagom

Lagom is often touted as the new Hygge. The similarities include focusing on contentment and simple living. However, the list of differences between the two lifestyles is a little longer.

Lagom is a Swedish word which means 'just the right amount'. The Lagom way of life requires you to do everything in moderation. It also includes taking just what is enough for you and leaving the rest for others.

So it wouldn't be wrong to say that Lagom is inspired by socialism. But since we're focusing on a moderate approach, we're expected to neither be too selfish nor too selfless. The lifestyle is about being realistic, just, and finding happiness in what you have.

Let's simplify this through an example. Imagine going to a sale where warm clothes are being sold at half the original price. Now, we all know that the stock items on sale are usually limited.

So let's say you like two sweaters for yourself. You can afford both but you only need one for the season. Therefore, instead of getting greedy or selfish, you only purchase one and be content with it.

This is what Lagom is all about. You think about not depriving others of their share of something good. You only take a reasonable amount of the things you require.

This rule doesn't only apply to people, but it extends to things, the society, the environment, and the planet as a whole. You care about yourself but you also care equally about the others. That is how you become a responsible citizen of the world.

Now talking about the aspect of moderation in everything, let's consider another example. We all know that sugar is not too good for health. Its long-term use has been linked to unhealthy weight gain and medical conditions like high blood pressure, diabetes, liver disease, etc.

But if you're living the Lagom lifestyle, you'll never resort to extreme measures. Hence, instead of giving up sugar completely, and at once, you gradually reduce the intake. You use it once in a while and keep the quantity in check as well.

Although we used this example to explain the concept of moderation in Lagom, it also sheds light on another important point. Whenever you quit a habit you're addicted to abruptly, you experience severe withdrawal symptoms. You feel like you've been deprived of something important.

With Lagom, you're less likely to feel so lost. The lifestyle that we currently lead is nothing short of an addiction. We simply can't do without upgrading all our facilities as frequently as we possibly can.

Transitioning to Lagom would not require you to abandon all the luxuries. But it would definitely allow you to set your limits and draw a line to the extravagance. You'll think more about the needs instead of the wants.

Sometimes, we start competing with our peers for a more lavish lifestyle. At others, we just can't resist the temptation to buy the newest model of our favorite brand of cars or mobile phones. Either way, we're just running after something or the other instead of being content with what we have.

As discussed in the text above, Lagom helps address such lifestyle issues. Now, to amalgamate Lagom with cocooning, we need to think of ways to find happiness without overdoing anything. We don't need to revamp our entire house to feel better.

Making small changes that bring you joy is more in line with this lifestyle. You're not prohibited from doing things that you enjoy as long as you do them in moderation. At the same time, you should avoid indulging in extravagance just for the sake of enjoyment.

Niksen

There are several meditational practices that require you to just side idle and cleanse your mind of all the thoughts. Such exercises provide a few moments of peace amid all the chaos. But just a few peaceful moments prove immensely helpful in restoring your mental health.

Niksen is just about having those few peaceful moments. It is like a breath of fresh air in your busy routine. But what it requires you to do is an even more interesting piece of information.

The Niksen lifestyle requires you to sit idle and do nothing. Sounds like the perfect kind of cocooning, doesn't it? Here's what it actually means.

If you're a workaholic, you always have an impending task on your mind. Even when you sit down to relax, your mind isn't completely free of worries. Such relaxation is quite futile and doesn't serve the purpose of re-energizing your mind and body.

Due to the environment that we're used to, most of us are overthinkers. Even while reading this, you wouldn't simply be absorbing the information. You would be connecting the dots and making comparisons simultaneously.

Niksen is a Dutch concept that means 'doing nothing'. You may have a million things to do but when you sit idle, none of those things should cross your mind. For example, the kitchen tap may need to get repaired but right now, if you're looking out of the window at two sparrows fighting over a piece of bread, you just stand there as a mere spectator.

No thoughts should flow in and out of your mind, you shouldn't contemplate anything philosophical and you definitely shouldn't worry. For those few moments, you just exist. Not every activity needs to consume all of your energy.

This is just like emptying a jug full of unused water so that fresh water can be poured in. You vacate the mind to make room for new and improved ideas. Luckily, with cocooning, Niksen is not so hard to incorporate into your lifestyle.

However, it's not so easy to actually master the art of 'doing nothing'. No matter what you do, you end up thinking about something or the other. The human mind does not have a switch that can be turned on or off at your convenience.

Sometimes you succeed in stopping the thought process and just staying idle. At other times you fail miserably as all the thoughts flood into your brain just as decide to keep your mind vacant for a bit. It's like the brain becomes as stubborn as you've been while over-exerting it for such a long time.

But the activity gets better with practice. Your stress levels go down significantly whenever you try it. So, having a few 'idle' moments everyday is definitely worth a shot.

Coorie

Coorie is just like the Scottish variant of Hygge. But there is one difference. The latest version of Coorie talks about 'embracing the outdoors' as well.
So you can't really make this a part of your cocooning. But you can definitely adopt the concept in its earlier, original form. Coorie simply means to snuggle or nestle.
Coorie is about enjoying all the Scottish traditions to attain a deep sense of happiness. The lifestyle pays particular attention to being close to nature and simple living. It involves going back to the basics to break the daily routine. Simple activities that help relieve stress like a family dinner, walk on a scenic track, sitting by the fire, etc can be considered the Coorie lifestyle. In order to stay indoors yet close to nature, you can decorate a corner of your house with plants and natural elements. Or you can just look at a scenery that makes you feel peaceful and happy. Nature has healing properties. So do a family's love and the company of good friends. No amount of artificial luxuries can replace the value that such things add to your life.

So the idea is to not have too many desires in order to feel happy. Just live simply and find contentment in the little joys that loved ones bring. Or if you're comfortable with your own company, you could just spend some time stargazing alone and that would be enough of refreshment for you.

———————

Hygge, Lagom, Niksen and Coorie: An overview

Every country adds its own colors to cocooning. There's no perfect or preferred way of the lifestyle. The choice is entirely personal.

You could even mix bits and pieces from different cultures to come up with your own unique form of cocooning. Staying indoors should bring you peace and not put you under stress about small details. The most important part is to decide that you'll create your own happiness in your own little cocoon.

Now all this discussion would seem like fancy wordplay if we don't answer the most important question: what activities can you try while cocooning? The above-mentioned lifestyles are more helpful in endorsing the right kind of attitude for cocooning. But you need to have some practical suggestions too.

It is insufficient to say 'stay happy indoors' until and unless we also elaborate on how that can be done. We wouldn't just direct you towards a bridge, we would like to help you cross it. So, in the next chapter, we discuss how you can make your cocooning experience more meaningful.

ACTIVITIES TO TRY AT HOME

The decision-making approach in life needs to be multi-dimensional. You can't just focus on one aspect and sacrifice everything else. Focusing on work alone would leave little time to look after your health and personal relationships. Similarly, being too concerned about your personal life would compromise the quality of your work.

Hence, one has to strike a balance between different responsibilities. These include professional responsibilities, personal responsibilities, and your responsibility to care for your mental, physical, and emotional wellbeing. Remember, we may often forget to include the last one in our checklist but we must learn to prioritize ourselves to improve our lifestyle.

When we make a life decision like choosing a job, moving to a new place, getting enrolled in a university program, etc, we consider a number of factors. These include considerations about finances, health, social affairs, entertainment choices, etc. So, when we are suggesting a lifestyle as unusual as cocooning, you may have a thousand questions in your mind. To address these, let's discuss some of the factors that may come into play while cocooning. You can take inspiration from here and add to the list of things to try while you are cocooning. There are several ways to improve this experience.

Productivity

There is a huge misconception that if you work from home, you may not be very productive or the quality of your work may decline. Those who believe this myth are of the view that sitting in one place every day can get monotonous and have a negative impact on your work. You may not feel motivated to work or may waste more time.

This is just incorrect information. Firstly, sitting in an office cubicle every day is also quite boring. There is no change in your surroundings and you can't make too many adjustments to your workplace.

Secondly, if your mind is at ease, working in isolation can be great for your productivity. Focusing on work away from all the unnecessary activities can only make you more efficient at it. So contrary to popular opinion, cocooning can actually enhance your productivity.

Practically every profession has room for remote operations these days. Barring work that requires manpower or physical assistance, everything can be done online. Although, there are exceptions (like surgeries and certain tests) but even healthcare providers are offering telemedicine services now.

At home, you have the liberty to create a workspace that makes work enjoyable. The idea of doing something productive should excite you and make you happy. Unlike (reluctantly) dragging your feet to the office every day, you should get up and look forward to starting work.

For this purpose, you can try different ideas like decorating your work desk to make it look more appealing. In offices, we're assigned a boring work cabin which adds to the monotony of our daily routine. At home, you have the liberty of experimenting with unique and creative ideas.

If you have a stable internet connection and a computer device, the rest is quite easy to mention. And these are facilities available in most households worldwide. In fact, you can have a global outreach for your business while operating from a small room in some remote part of the world.

Entertainment

All work and no play is not a healthy lifestyle choice either. You need to have an adequate amount of relaxation too. So when you're figuring out the ideal kind of lifestyle, make sure you pay attention to the entertainment choices available as well.

While cocooning, there's a variety of things that you can do to keep yourself entertained. For example, one of the main sources of entertainment (for many decades) has been going to the cinema to watch a movie. Cinema-goers eagerly wait for new movies to release so that they can enjoy them with friends or family.

But with the latest technology, this conventional method of entertainment has been completely transformed. Now you can enjoy instant access to a wide range of movies (from multiple genres) and have greater control over the kind of content you want. Service providers offer this facility at nominal rates worldwide.

If you don't like watching movies alone, you can plan weekly or monthly movie nights with your friends. This gathering at home proves to be even better than the experience at a theatre because you can enjoy greater comfort with just the right kind of company. You can even pause/rewind/forward certain parts or change the movie without requiring a ticket.

This is just one example of the things that you can do for entertainment in a cocooning lifestyle. But it provides a clear comparison between the comfort level associated with indoor and outdoor activities. The ease and convenience also apply to music, tv shows, video games, etc.

If you like reading, you can also build a small library in one part of the apartment/house. Of course, there are a number of virtual libraries where you can access thousands of books online. But somehow that experience doesn't feel as personal as having an old-style, conventional library at home does.

Besides, this little corner could be your own separate wonderland. You could read about history, fiction novels, or even simple 'how-to' books to increase your knowledge. Considered one of the most enriching experiences, reading books increases your knowledge and makes your problem-solving skills better.

Book lovers would agree that whenever they're reading a certain book, they enter into a different zone. The genre you're reading starts influencing your thoughts and actions. So reading a lot of positive content can be really good for your mental health.

Hobbies

People who attend dance classes regularly or who go for hiking or walks may wonder how they're going to continue these habits in cocooning. The answer lies yet again in technology. You can attend virtual classes or replace natural hikes with exercising equipment that provides a similar experience.

But instead of continuing the same old hobbies, cocooning should also be used to explore newer ones. We should try activities that are more relevant to this lifestyle. Time spent indoors can be greatly helpful in enhancing your skills.

Time spent at home should not feel like imprisonment. There is a cliched quote that reads something like 'home is where the heart is'. When you contemplate its meaning, you realize how well cocooning fits with this idea.

When a criminal is held captive for too long, even he/she starts doodling on the walls. The plain surroundings start bothering you too much after a while. Not that we're equating a comfortable home to a prison cell but when you know you'll be looking at the same four walls for a long while, you would obviously want your view to be pleasant.

Spending too much time at home will automatically make you better at interior design. You would want your home to look colorful, cozy, and well-maintained. A cheerful environment naturally uplifts your mood as well.

So this is a great hobby to have in cocooning. It might be helpful to know that some colors are generally associated with a better mood. You could use such information and ideas to further alleviate your stress woes.

Another hobby that lets you play with colors is painting. Your canvas may be smaller than it is while designing interiors but with your color palette you can use your imagination to make all sorts of designs. Even simple paintbrush strokes are quite fun and stress-relieving.

As we have already mentioned in an earlier part of the text, nature has healing properties. So hobbies like gardening are also in line with a stress-relieving, cocooning lifestyle. Staying close to plants, looking after them is a very healthy activity.

Similarly, cooking, sketching, yoga, etc, are all examples of hobbies that are good for your mental health. You don't even need much to get started with these at home. There are plenty of options to refresh your mind once you set your mind to it.

The internet is full of new and creative things that you can learn from home. The DIY tutorials are quite helpful in this regard. From arts and crafts to playing musical instruments, you can learn so much for free.

One thing that we must remember is that cocooning saves time spent traveling to and from work. It also saves the time and effort spent on other outdoor activities. This means you will have some spare time on your hands and you should plan to use it well.

Social life

When Buddha left everything behind and set out into the forest, he did not intend to return. He wanted to break all ties and focus on spirituality. He felt like the worldly matters did not let him focus on his conscience.

You may take inspiration from the idea of detaching yourself from your surroundings to attain a higher level of spirituality. However, you do not have to do something as drastic as Buddha did. You're expected to limit social gatherings, not give up on the idea completely.

In cocooning, you're not required to sever ties with everybody. Attending less outdoor events does not mean you also can't invite your loved ones at home for a nice meal from time to time. In fact, such activities are actually encouraged in this lifestyle.

Not seeing friends and family at all is also not beneficial for your mental health. We need to look after our social needs as well. After all, you wouldn't want to step out of one stressful situation into another.

You can plan simple cozy evenings to play card games, board games, or even video games with friends and family. Alternatively, if you have enough space at home, you can make arrangements for a sports activity whenever you have some company. For example, getting table tennis equipment or a snooker table placed in some part of the house is not difficult these days.

Just like individual activities that we talked about earlier, there are plenty of group activities to try in cocooning. Whenever the lifestyle starts to seem a bit lonely, you can quickly call up a friend and plan something fun. Remember, we're focusing on happiness and contentment in this lifestyle and anything that makes you feel miserable should be changed immediately.

Quite often in our lives, we hold ourselves back from acting a certain way. For example, we may not like to be the first one to call or message for the fear of judgment from the other person. Due to such self-imposed restrictions, we often end up feeling suffocated.

The lifestyle change that we're suggesting may involve staying indoors mostly but in reality, it is the most liberating experience. You only do what you deem best for your happiness. Not caring about what other people think or feel lifts a heavy burden off your chest.

So, in terms of social life, cocooning meets you'll only meet the people you want, at the time you want and as often as you like. You get to decide whether you want a quiet evening with some good food or a dance party with all of your friends invited. When you truly put your heart and soul into spending quality time with your guests, your company becomes dearer to other people as well.

This is how cocooning improves the quality of your social relationships as well. People look forward to meeting you. Personally, with a greater level of mental peace, you become a better listener and can be there for other people too.

Cocooning lifestyle: a summary

Throughout this text, we have highlighted the various aspects of the cocooning lifestyle. We have also mentioned quite a few benefits that it provides. But the positive effect it has on a person's mental health cannot be overemphasized.

Think of this as a retreat to a comfortable and mood-lifting place. So far we have been discussing how you can create such an environment at home and what it really means. Now let's try to imagine what really happens once you're in that safe zone.

A bird builds its nest with a lot of hard work. It keeps adding one straw after the other until there is a comfortable place to live in. This nest is its protection from other animals, severe weather, and all kinds of harsh environments.

After flying here and there throughout the day, it comes back to the nest to rest. The period when you're setting up your place for cocooning is similar to the bird building its nest. A beautiful, cozy, and peaceful place where you can just relax.

When the home is ready, and you start living the cocooning way, consider this a peaceful night after a long and tiring day. By long and tiring day, we mean all the years that you've spent hustling. Considering how anxious this lifestyle has been, you deserve a long period of rest.

During this time, your home will be your empire. But you would be the kind of ruler who believes in adding value to life rather than chest-thumping or creating a show. In other words, a ruler that believes in simple living.

Now, coming back to the topic of mental health. Firstly, the feeling of having greater control over your life makes you more at ease. It helps in reducing stress and anxiety.

Moreover, setting your own routine, doing things that you love improves your emotional health. You feel more motivated and cheerful. This also reflects in your overall health.

Lastly, the kind of interactions that may make you uncomfortable are minimized. So there is a lesser chance of developing issues like social anxiety. It is much easier to handle stressful situations virtually.

At the beginning of this text, we mentioned the most widely known meaning of the word cocoon. It refers to the protective covering that many insects build around themselves. The human concept of cocooning also derives its meaning from this.

Now, at the end of the text, we would like to make a particular reference to the cocoons of silkworms. Silk is one of the most luxurious clothes in the work. It is obtained from the silky case spun by silkworms.

The reason to mention this again here is to point out that something so beautiful comes from a cocoon. In the latest terminology, if the human house can also be called a cocoon, we can only imagine amazing results from this practice. There might not be much evidence available as yet but as the trend becomes older, we will come to realize many more long-lasting benefits of cocooning.

We can't change everything that is happening in the world. For example, climate change is a serious problem and is expected to get worse in the coming years. There will be harsh weather patterns in all seasons everywhere.

Outdoor weather is something that is beyond our control. We can't change the severity of the weather outside. Neither would getting worried about it be of any help.

But what we can do is create a cozy, comfortable environment indoors. This will keep us functional and happy. Our routine matter won't be disturbed because of the weather.

To summarize the entire discussion, it would suffice to say that the lifestyle is greatly helpful in improving the quality of your life. A well-rested, content, and peaceful person makes much better progress in all areas of life. Cocooning helps you achieve all three of these objectives.

CONCLUSION

Have you ever thought about the reason that the idea of camping seems so exciting? You're just living in a tent with minimal facilities. There are no concrete buildings or proper infrastructure around.

The reason is, it feels like an escape from the everyday routine. A routine that involves noise, machinery, crowds, etc. The human mind is not designed mechanically. It needs a nourishing environment to function properly for a longer period of time.

This is what cocooning and similar lifestyles are aimed at achieving. As you would have realized by now, it is not a very difficult idea to implement. Whichever part of it seems like a nuisance or doesn't serve your purpose can be purpose as per your choice.

The global lifestyle trends are continuously evolving according to the changing times. All the tasks and activities are being adjusted to make the people more self-reliant. While inter-dependence is a great social concept, it isn't too helpful in more practical matters.

People are increasingly becoming self-employed. Houses are being designed to allow for a greater number of indoor activities. Moreover, societies are being constructed with the main focus being sustainability.

People are increasingly becoming self-employed. Houses are being designed to allow for a greater number of indoor activities. Moreover, societies are being constructed with the main focus being sustainability.

Just like the aforementioned examples, day to day habits are being changed for the better. There is a greater awareness about the needs of the mind and body among people. Along with ideas like preserving the environment and the planet, they're also more concerned about preserving their own mental peace.

Staying indoors does not even necessarily mean being secluded anymore. A person who has not left home for a long time may know a lot more about the outside world as compared to a person who commutes to work daily. It is all about staying well-connected to the rest of the world regardless of your physical movement.

Speaking of connections, you can't truly connect to anybody or anything in the world until and unless you're deeply connected to your inner self. Cocooning provides enough stability to remind yourself of the things that really matter in life. It gives you time to regroup your energies.

Safety is the first and foremost consideration whenever you're starting something new. When combined with happiness, it creates an ideal situation for any person. That's what we're suggesting with the title of this text, to enjoy both safety and happiness by adopting the cocooning lifestyle.

When the world becomes too noisy, it is time to go back into your hiding and observe everything quietly. Trying to participate in every debate and discussion will only leave you tired and frustrated. The same is the case with outdoor activities. Participating in too many is not favorable for your mind and body.

We've all often heard that we should choose our battles wisely. But we should also include other choices (that should be made carefully) in this list. This would include how much and what kind of company we need, what makes us happy, and what kind of lifestyle do we want to live.

More Books by Tess Jansen

Niksen: The Power Of Doing NOTHING

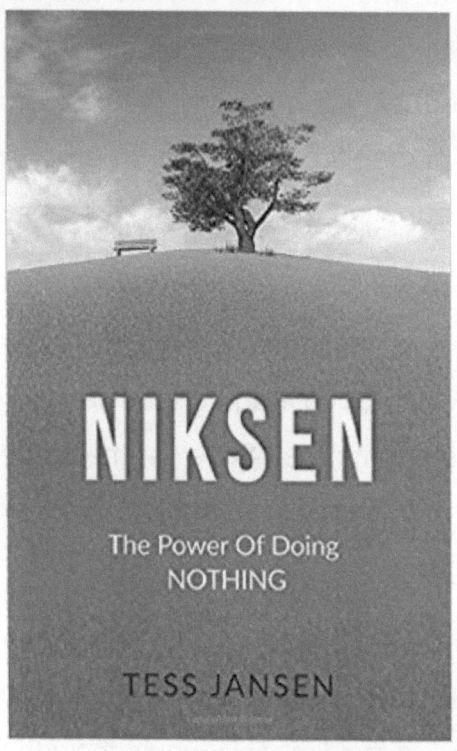

Nordic Lifestyle Trends: Niksen & Friluftsliv

www.ingramcontent.com/pod-product-compliance
Lightning Source LLC
LaVergne TN
LVHW040201080526
838202LV00042B/3266